A Little Light

By

Akpomah Nelson Mandella

Love Profits

My story will teach you the course to help every child in need because they are still the future of our existence.

This is a true life story of a boy whom at his early age has no parent yet his existence was centered on love and care.

The story will build your mental strength to helping people because even the world lacks the ability to tell what tomorrow will bring.

My name is Rufus Badmus and this was how it began.

The beginning of my life was a ferry tail, just like the fish that lived without water.

My parents were very young and they got married at the ages of 20 and 17 respectively. Upon my birth, my both parents died and they left me in this dangerous place called the earth.

I came into the world at about 1:30am on the 19th of August, 1997 which was told to me by my mother's friend Mrs Anita Chima.

To further explain how my parent died, Mrs Anita Chima told me that my mother died giving birth to me and because of the incident my father also passed away after taking care of me for 3 months.

And this was the beginning of my dark days.

The dark days of my life started at the age of 3 months till the day I became 25.

Without anyone to call daddy or mommy is the worst state for a child.

My story will teach you the course to help every child in need because they are still the future of our existence.

At the age 3 to 4 months my life started to sail like a ship without a captain.

I was taken by my parent neighbours; I was tossed around from one house to another because no family wants an additional liability.

Really it was a tussle amongst them all, because of the rate of poverty in the environment. Eating three times a day is a luxury to the neighbour; talk more of adding a child whose needs are more complex than just making food.

Mrs Anita Chima who told me about my life and how I became an adult was the part to my success because she always tell me about my parents good deeds and how they where loved by all.

I lived with the neighbours for 10 years and I never knew who amongst the neighbours was my parent because I call them daddy and mommy.

On my 10th birthday the neighbour host a party to celebrate my life and also said some things about my parents which made me sad and those words influenced my leaving the environment without letting anyone know my where about.

This step of mine was like a bicycle trying to climb a hill, before I left I took a lot of food that was made at the party and snacks too with a lot of sweets and chocolates.

It took me three days to get to a different town on foot and because I did not know where I was going at that time. It was a hell of pain and agony.

When I entered the town, it was different from what I use to know because everyone was busy doing their own thing without concern for the other. After a few hours the Rain began to pour heavily and I hard to look for a shelter.

Running and looking for shelter In a place you have no clue about their culture and behaviour at the age of 10 was a thing i still find pondering about till this day.

With the mind of getting a shelter I ran into a woman's shop and with anger she shouted saying "who is this thing in my shop, where you sent, will you get out of my shop?"

So I ran out of the woman's shop and ran opposite the shop I came out of to a ladies shop with hope that I will not be asked to leave the shop again.

Luckily the lady called and said "boy; where is your mother and why are you in the rain all by yourself?" before I could answer she dragged me into the shop and gave me dry towel to keep me dry.

At the same instance she asked if I hard eating and with no replies she brought me some rice and stew and sat me down to eat.

With the shock of how the first woman treated me I was still not convinced that the lady who was helping me really meant what she was doing.

Then the lady said finish eating and rest ok, I replied ok. That was the first word that came out of my mouth in over 45 minutes or an hour.

After I finished eating I slept off on the chair I was sitting, I never knew how I get to the ladies house that day until I woke up the next morning.

That morning when I woke up I saw the lady starring at me sitting beside me on the bed.

With a wonderful smile she said good morning to you boy, what is your name?

My name is Rufus Badmus.
where are your parents? She
asked; I don't have a
parent.....

So I asked her madam,
please what is your name
and where are your children?

She smiled at me saying "I
don't have children, am not
married, my name is Miss
Jennifer Moses, I leave alone
hear".

So I said, In this big house. She replied saying "it's me and you now, or will you not like to stay with me here?"

This was how "A Little Light" shined on me.

From that day on I began a new routing on what I do every day and also follow Miss Jennifer to her shop, as time passes I began to call her mother and this happened because of her care and love.

She was one of the kindest ladies I have ever meet, she thought me so much that she made me become like her and scold me for every wrong on my part,

she was a mother.

She started teaching me the ways of her life and how to leave without any support from anyone.

She got me into school months later and from then on I started living like I really have a family for some years.

My time is school was also strange just like every other student who will get to school for the first time seeing new faces and new people just like every other student. But one thing was different because I was sitting alone in the classroom while others sits I three.

The darkness that loomed after me during my stay at my parent neighbourhood started falling around me again, this time it was very hash with so many mysterious happenings that I could not understand or believe should happened.

First, when I was introduced to the class I was laughed at and that gave me concerns because I never knew what the problem was or what I have done that was funny to them all.

Do to this the teacher asked me to sit on her sit and asked that they bring me a chair and a table, after some minutes the chair and table was brought to me and then I started sitting alone.

To me, I told myself to always be alone so that I don't get into trouble with the other students.

Because of this I never speak to anyone or ask for anything so as to stay out of trouble but somehow the problems and troubles I run from just keep chasing me.

This issue of darkness chasing me became intense when we finish the first term examination.

I became the best in the class and every other student in the class where furious about it and from then on they kept bullying and plotting things that could make me leave the school.

The next term began and the rivalry continued, this time I told my New mother (Miss Jennifer Moses) what has been happening since the day I entered school. But her words to me gave me more life than I already have. She said "if you have stayed for a term and you are still living then they are only making you stronger my boy".

When I got to school the next day I was called upon by the Head master at the assembly ground to come out, when I did, the head master told me that I was reported to have stolen a textbook from a student's bag. At first I was dumfounded by the head masters words and then I replied saying "no sir I never took any text book from anyone".

The entire student at the assembly shouted "thief....thief....thief...." and so it continued, then I was asked to go to the head masters office and kneel down.

After the school assemble
was over they called my
mother (Miss Jennifer Moses)
to come to the school
because I have done
something wrong.

With the curiosity of every mother she lucked up her shop and ran straight to the school, when she got to the head master office she saw me kneeling down. She screamed at me say "my boy what have you done?" So the head master asked her to sit down so that she can understand the full story behind my kneeling down.

After a few minutes with the head master, my mother came out and started screaming on top of her voice saying "my son can ever do something of such, I want to see the person who reported my child", the situation was becoming so tensed and everyone was agitated by it.

In the middle of the chaos my class teacher eventually came with the student who reported me to the head master. The head master asked everyone to sit down so as to get to the bottom of the issue and to resolve it at once.

When everyone was settled, the head master asked the disciplinary teachers to start up with their measures to sieve out the truth from the student.

So it began; Daniel they called the student, did you know Rufus Badmus? He replied and said yes sir, he is my classmate, why did you report him of stealing your textbook, he replied that he was told by Favour another of my classmate that Rufus was the one that stole the textbook.

When my mother hard this she quickly asked Daniel, did you ask Rufus about the textbook before you reported to the head master? He said no.

So the disciplinary teachers asked my class teacher to call Favour for questioning.

When favour arrived at the head teachers office she was so scared with the way everyone was looking at her. Then they asked her to sit and she did.

One of the disciplinary teachers now asked Favour if she knew Daniel and Rufus (me), she answer saying yes, they are my classmates.

The disciplinary teacher asked Favour again, did you tell Daniel that you saw Rufus taking his textbook?

She said no but she told Daniel that he saw me leaving the classroom last, so she concluded that it was Rufus who stole to textbook.

Then my mother quickly asked her again Favour; did you see my son taking the book? She said no.

Then Daniel said; Favour told him and Julius another classmate of ours that she saw him taking the textbook. Eventually they had to call for Julius who was said to be a witness to this issue.

As usual the questions were asked if Julius knew us all and he replied saying; yes they are my classmates.

The second question this time was direct from the disciplinary teachers; did Favour tell you and Daniel that she saw Rufus taking any textbook from anyone's bag?

Julius was so direct and specific with his words saying; she came to us at the playing field where we were watching the final match between primary 5 and primary 6 and told us that she saw Rufus taking Daniels textbook.

So we ran straight to the classroom but could not find the textbook, out of anger Daniel went straight to the head master and reported the issue and that was it.

After that was side I was asked to stand up and go back to class, Julius and Daniel where also asked to leave.

Favour was then asked to wait for her parents to come and my mother hard to wait too until the issue was finally resolved.

Favour was expelled from the school and from that day on till I finished my primary classes I was never bullied by anyone again.

The love of my mother towards me increased so much that I never believed cared so much about my well being.

In my final examination at the primary class I became the best student that ever came to the school.

I was given a scholarship by the school to stay and resume their secondary classes. I will attend the junior classes for free, without paying any fee.

When I got home and passed the message to my mother, she was so excited and promised to get me some new bag and textbooks for me resumption.

It was time for the new section to begin after two months of holiday. I took my old uniform and my new bag and went to school because I have no uniforms for the junior class yet.

The principal of the school called me and asked me to go to the staff room and get my uniform, I was very happy because everything I need from the school will be free.

From my first year to the third year at the junior class was a very successful and wonderful moments of my life. My result was excellent and most of the students where those at my primary class too.

Resumption for the senior class began and this time almost half of my former classmates have changed their schools for one reason or another. In the class we were all strange to each other because the new students were trying to make friends why some are not.

During this time I hard to stay away from others because I don't want to be a victim to any form of incident that would lead to expulsion.

I managed to cope through all the issues from the classes and teachers too.

When I got to the final year of graduation, we wrote the examinations as usual, with joy I was hoping to pass all my papers because everything about the examination was very easy for anyone who took time to read their books.

The next day when I came to school I was told that some of my answer scripts where not submitted, at first I was just surprised then I replied saying; I submitted all my answer scripts, how is it possible for my answer script to be left out?

So I quickly picked up the scripts and found out that these scripts where actually mine and the subjects where English, Mathematics and Book of Accounting. All these were my most important subjects.

When I got home I told my mother about the issue and she told me not to worry because sometimes our plans for life are not the plans for God Almighty. She said my son you are the best student in my class and beyond so don't worry yourself over all these ok.

Few weeks later the results for the examinations where out and I failed the three subjects that were not submitted. Due to this I could not further my education and started selling at the shop with my mother.

A year has passed with me still helping my mother at the shop where she sells. One evening a man came in to the shop dressed in tattered cloths and came to me saying; sir, please am hungry and I don't have money can you please give me food?

I asked him to have a sit and went in to get him food, before I came back the man was off the chair and I went outside to look left and right to see if I would see him but my search for him was to no avail.

After some minutes, the man was back requesting for the food but this he was dressed in a wine coloured suit and a sky blue shirt with a nice shiny black shoes. I was confused of what to say or what to do at that point.

So I immediately brought the food to him and he ate every bit of the food and said thank you. Then he said to me "are you busy? If not please have a sit".

So I took off the dishes from the table and then sat down. He went beneath the table and took up a brief case with a silver colour; it was so clean and shiny like a diamond.

Then he said to me; my names are Mr Kelvin Gibson, I am the CEO of Alpha Bykings oil and gas Fuel station.

Out of anxiety I shouted OMG!! Are you serious sir, why did you have to pretend to be a nobody?

He answered and I have been doing this for days now and everyone keep chasing me away, you where the only person who asked me to sit down. For that reason you will be the owner of all my companies around the country.

I shouted again OMG!! With tear all over me, then he said open the brief case, when I did, I found hundreds of dollar, I quickly called my mother to come over to the shop.

When she came she saw me crying, she rushed at me thinking I was hurt, but the man said to her, madam please let him be; that is tears of joy. She was still not convinced so she dragged me up and wiped my face with her wrapper and said my son please talk to me.

Without any words I opened the brief case and she saw the money and fainted. When she woke up Mr Kelvin Gibson has already left.

With the right state of mind my mother asked me saying; who gave me that money? So I told him it was Mr Kelvin Gibson the CEO of Alpha Bykigs oil and gas fuel station.

When I told her the whole story, My mother said to me my son, did you remember what I told you about Gods plan and that of man? I answered say yes mother I did. She then said, you see now; "A little light" has shine beyond your imagination.

This is what God Almighty can do.

From that day on I became one of the richest persons within the continent.